THOMAS KINKADE

BEACONS OF LIGHT

light

Thomas Kinkade
Beacons of Light

**Andrews McMeel
Publishing**

Kansas City

For information, write Andrews McMeel Publishing, an Andrews McMeel Universal company, 4520 Main Street, Kansas City, Missouri 64111.

ISBN: 0-7407-4260-4

Library of Congress Catalog Card Number: 2004101336

www.thomaskinkade.com

Compiled by Patrick Regan

*L*ight truly has the POWER *to* ILLUMINATE *our* LIVES *and* GUIDE *us* home.

$\mathcal{M}$any's the sea captain who has rejoiced at the sight of an illuminated lighthouse on a distant shore. For hundreds of years, such stoic, reliable beacons have led wayward travelers to sanctuary.

$\mathcal{E}$ven if we never see the world's vast oceans, each of us faces times in life when we feel adrift. In those times when we're weary and sailing on unkind waters, we seek out a safe harbor.

$\mathcal{B}$ut we need not drift on rough waters forever—for even in times of darkness and doubt, there are always bastions of hope and beacons of light to guide us. For some, the light is a powerful friendship, for others, a strong family, and for many, the guiding light comes from an unshakable faith in God.

$\mathcal{A}$s a painter and as a person, I believe in the overwhelming power of light. Whether the strong lighthouse beam cutting through thick fog or the warm glow of firelight emanating from a cottage window, light fills us with hope, warmth, and serenity. Light truly has the power to illuminate our lives and guide us home.

THOMAS KINKADE

***L**ight is the* SYMBOL *of* TRUTH.

—James Russell Lowell

THE
Foundations
of a PERSON *are not*
IN *matter*
but in SPIRIT.

—Ralph Waldo Emerson

With *every* CREATIVE ACT, *you* LIGHT *a fresh candle for a* DARKENED WORLD—*and that in itself is a* POWERFUL *source of joy for your* LIFE.

—Thomas Kinkade

FAITH
is like
ELECTRICITY.
You can't SEE *it,*
but you can SEE
the LIGHT.

—Anonymous

Man is
so MADE *that*
when
anything
FIRES *his*
SOUL,
impossibilities
vanish.

—Jean de La Fontaine

light

Your life can

RADIATE

the kind of light that truly makes a

DIFFERENCE

in the

WORLD.

—Thomas Kinkade

*I*t *is* TRULY said: It does not take much STRENGTH *to* do things, but it REQUIRES great strength to decide what *to* DO.

—Chow Ching

*M*ost of us, swimming AGAINST *the tides of* TROUBLE *the world knows nothing about, need only a bit of* PRAISE *or* ENCOURAGEMENT—*and we will make the* GOAL.

—Jerome P. Fleishman

*W*hen *you*
LIVE *in the*
LIGHT *of*
unfolding
MIRACLES, *there*
is always a
FUTURE, *always*
a HOPE.

—Thomas Kinkade

No WINTER *lasts* *forever; no* SPRING *skips* *its turn.*

—Hal Borland

Appreciation of LIFE itself, becoming suddenly aware of the MIRACLE of being ALIVE, on this planet, can TURN what we call ORDINARY life into a MIRACLE. We come AWAKE to such a REALIZATION when we recognize our CONNECTION to a SPIRITUAL dimension.

—Dan Wakefield

When I see my LIFE *as a series of unfolding* MIRACLES, *I'll always sail forth with* HOPE, TRANQUILLITY, *and* JOY *in my heart.*

—Thomas Kinkade

Not
FARE *well,*
but fare
FORWARD,
voyagers.

—T. S. Eliot

Cherish your VISIONS;
cherish your IDEALS;
*cherish the music
that stirs in your heart,
the* BEAUTY *that forms in your* MIND,
the LOVELINESS *that drapes your
purest* THOUGHTS . . .
*if you but remain true to them,
your world will at last be built.*

—James Allen

trust

*F*aith is the CHOICE *to sail* FORWARD *before you are sure why you are going through what you are going through . . . before you are* CONFIDENT *you can* TRUST *the final outcome.*

—Thomas Kinkade

Beautiful LIGHT *is born* *of* DARKNESS, *so the* FAITH *that springs* *from conflict is* *often the* STRONGEST *and the* BEST.

—R. Turnbull

The power in which we must have faith if we would be well, is the

CREATIVE
and
CURATIVE
power which exists in every living thing.

—John Kellogg

HOPE

will HELP *you find your way through* DARK *and* STORMY *nights . . . through* FOGGY *and* CONFUSING *days.*

—Thomas Kinkade

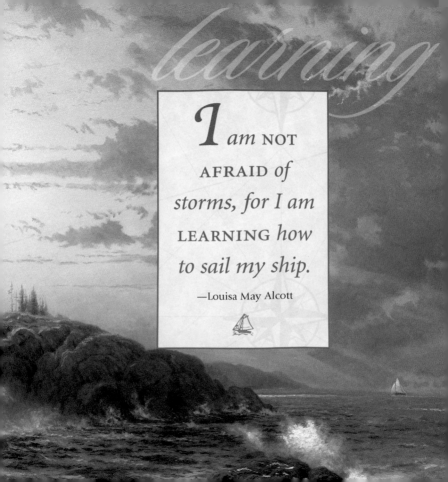

learning

I *am* NOT
AFRAID *of*
storms, for I am
LEARNING *how*
to sail my ship.

—Louisa May Alcott

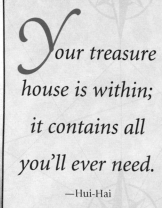

Your treasure house is within; it contains all you'll ever need.

—Hui-Hai

Once we
DISCOVER *how*
to appreciate
the timeless
VALUES *in*
our daily
EXPERIENCES,
we can enjoy
the best things
in LIFE.

—Harry Hepner

MAKE
Time
IN YOUR *Life*
FOR
Wonder.

—Thomas Kinkade

Thomas Kinkade

Spirit is
MATTER *seen*
in a stronger
LIGHT.

—L. P. Jacks

believe

IBELIEVE _though I_
do not
COMPREHEND,
and I hold by
FAITH _what_
I cannot
GRASP _with_
the MIND.

—St. Bernard

*There are two ways
of spreading light:
to be the candle
or the mirror
that reflects it.*

—Edith Wharton

Cherish the

PEOPLE *who make* *up your* **HOME,** *and you'll notice the hearth* **FIRES** *burn* **BRIGHTER** *than ever before.*

—Thomas Kinkade

home

Thomas Kinkade

I have come
back again to
where I
BELONG; *not an*
ENCHANTED
place, but the
walls are
STRONG.

—Dorothy H. Rath

*T*he WISEST *keeps something of the*
VISION *of a child. Though he may*
UNDERSTAND *a thousand things that*
a child could not UNDERSTAND,
he is always a beginner, close to the
ORIGINAL MEANING *of life.*

—John Macy

Path

You will RECOGNIZE *your own* PATH *when you come upon it, because you will suddenly have all the*

ENERGY

and

IMAGINATION

you will ever need.

—Jerry Gillies

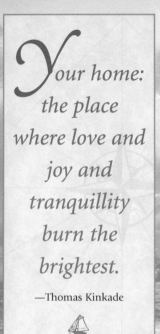

*Y*our home:
the place
where love and
joy and
tranquillity
burn the
brightest.

—Thomas Kinkade

The

STRENGTH *of a*
nation derives
from the
INTEGRITY *of*
the HOME.

—Confucius

Hope

Hope
is the parent
of faith.

—Cyrus A. Bartol

When you cannot make up your mind which of two evenly BALANCED *courses of* ACTION *you should take—choose the* BOLDER.

—William Joseph Slim

Reason

The way to see by Faith is to shut the Eye of Reason.

—Benjamin Franklin

*I*f you find that JOY *is fading in* *your* HEART, *you might pay* attention to your PASSIONS, *your* PURPOSES, *and* *your* PURSUITS.

—Thomas Kinkade

passion

Thomas
Kinkade

glory

I see
heaven's
glories shine
and faith
shines equal.

—Emily Brontë

CREATIVITY, *as has been said,* *consists largely of* REARRANGING *what we* KNOW *in order to find out* *what we do not know. Hence, to* *think* CREATIVELY, *we must be able* *to look afresh at what we normally* *take for granted.*

—George Kneller

Thomas Kinkade

*S*URROUND *yourself with the kinds of input that are* UPLIFTING, *that* EXPAND *your* MIND *and* SETTLE *your* SPIRIT.

—Thomas Kinkade

*B*elief
consists in
ACCEPTING *the*
affirmations of
the SOUL;
UNBELIEF, *in*
DENYING *them.*

—Ralph Waldo Emerson

WHAT YOU KEEP TO
YOURSELF YOU LOSE;
WHAT YOU
GIVE
AWAY, YOU
KEEP
FOREVER.

—Axel Munthe

reflect

Thomas
Kinkade

*O*nly let the moving waters CALM down, and the sun and moon will be REFLECTED on the surface of your BEING.

—Jal'al al-D'in Rumi

It's the highest CALLING *any of us have in life: making the* WORLD *a little* BRIGHTER *because of the way we paint our* DAYS *and* HOURS *and* MONTHS *and* YEARS.

—Thomas Kinkade

W are

what we

BELIEVE *we are.*

—Benjamin N. Cardozo

give

*T*he most
satisfying thing
in life is to have
been able to
give a large
part of oneself
to others.

—Pierre Teilhard de Chardin

$\mathcal{Y}$our life has meaning and
beauty, and you are not in it alone.

—Thomas Kinkade